Bamboozled
by a Bobcat

A Louisiana Boy's Dirt Road Recollections

Bamboozled by a Bobcat

A Louisiana Boy's Dirt Road Recollections

by

Glynn Harris

Bamboozled by a Bobcat: A Louisiana Boy's Dirt Road Recollections

© 2023 by Glynn Harris

Published in Ruston, Louisiana.

Cover Design by Victoria Davies (vikncharlie on Fiverr.com)
Interior Design by Morgan Tarpley Smith (morgantarpleysmith.com/services)

Front & Back Cover Photography provided by Glynn Harris
Shown in front cover photo (from left): Glynn, his father, and brother, Tom.

Scripture quotations are taken from the King James Version.

Printed in the United States of America
2023—First Edition

Endorsements

"And when he picks one out to write about it and you read it, you feel like you've been there with him the whole way. I swear one time after reading one of his tales about catching and cleaning some big old bluegill bream, I thought I could smell fish on my own hands.

Whether he's writing about 'moonshine' in the church, guitar picking or his vast love of the outdoors, his authentic thoughts and downhome style are just what the doctor ordered to get your mind away from this wacky world for a few minutes. And, as a fellow outdoor writer I can say without question, all Glynn's stories are absolutely true. At least they start out that way. I'm sure you'll enjoy his book and the stories inside."

—Kinny Haddox, editor of Louisiana Sportsman

"I have been a fan of Glynn Harris, and of his award-winning writing and his picking, for many years. That makes reading (this book) a special treat...a back-porch conversation with a gentle and talented soul whose prose and music both make the world better. It's a chance to walk with him through a childhood from another era, through the carefree days of summer and the chill of winter, with nature, faith, and all the good country cooking a mother could whip up as the backdrop. This is a memoir for relaxing with, and it is as welcome a companion as he is."

—Rob Simbeck, former president of the Southeastern Outdoor Press Association and author of "The Southern Wildlife Watcher"

"Glynn Harris is a man of all seasons. Hunting season. Fishing season. Guitar pickin' season. From Goldonna Baptist to the Dixie Theater to the KXKZ radio studios to any patch of North Louisiana woods you can shake a shotgun at, Glynn Harris has made the rounds — and not out of duty, but out of joy and a love of life. Enjoy spending some time with Glynn through these joy-infused stories — and be glad you're not a squirrel or dove or deer in his range."

—Teddy Allen, award-winning sports writer and columnist, 2022 Louisiana Sports Hall of Fame inductee

"Glynn Harris' 'Bamboozled by a Bobcat: A Louisiana Boy's Dirt Road Recollections' takes the reader on a heartfelt journey through a life richly lived. With tales ranging from 'moon-shine' mishaps in the church house to the author's fervent love affair with the guitar, these recollections are woven together with a tapestry of outdoor adventures, hunting escapades, and the evolution of a budding writer. Through Harris' always-engaging storytelling, readers are invited to participate in his experiences, finding humor, nostalgia, and inspiration in every carefully crafted word. Buy you a copy now but don't start reading it until you have some time on your hands. You won't put it down until you've read it start to finish!"

—Keith "Catfish" Sutton with C&C Outdoor Productions Inc. and editor of CatfishNow Magazine

Dedicated to my high school English teacher:
my aunt, Lillian Montgomery,
who was extra tough on me because she saw something that
indicated my potential as a writer

Table of Contents

Growing Up

I was fortunate growing up.

Our home consisted of four rooms and a *path*. No indoor plumbing at first. I have vague memories of our house being built by a group of fellows including my dad. We were living temporarily with my grandparents while the house was being built next door. It was like a square box with four rooms of equal dimensions—living room, kitchen, two bedrooms. That was it. Later, front and back porches were added, and even later after we got electricity and had a deep well drilled, we had a bathroom.

On the front porch was our *porch swing* and a couple of rocking chairs where we'd sit in the late evenings. Mother taught us about things like seeing the first star and catching lightning bugs and during the day teaching us to identify the birds in our yard. Daddy taught us manly stuff like hunting and fishing, but it was Mother who introduced us to the "soft side" of the outdoors.

The back porch that was later added held a daybed which provided some fine sleeping on hot summer nights. Later after we got electricity, we bought a deep freeze that stayed on the back porch. Also, Mother's washing machine was there— an old wringer washer, and since there was no dryer, Mother used a clothesline in the backyard where our clothes were hung after being washed.

When it was *coming up a cloud*, we had to hurry and get the clothes off the line before they got wet. I still remember the fresh clean smell of clothes when they came in off the clothesline. Before hanging the clothes on the line, there was a wash tub for rinse water that was out in the yard. We often used the tub of water for our Saturday night baths. Since I was the oldest, I usually got to take my bath first, and Tom would have to bathe in my bath water. I think he sorta resented that.

We finally got a phone before I left home for college, and we were on a party line. Our number was simply 5184. We were on the party line with several other families, and our ring was two short rings. That's when we would answer the phone. Others had three short rings, one long and one short and so forth. It wasn't unusual to be talking and hear another phone pick up on the party line. Somebody was snooping and listening in.

With only two bedrooms, it was necessary for my brother, Tom, and me to sleep together. In summer, we were too hot with no air conditioner or fan. We lived along a gravel road, and during hot summer nights, I remember the smell and even taste of the red dirt dust hanging in the air.

In winter, Mother piled on quilts to the extent it was hard to turn over, but we needed them to keep warm. Mother would sometimes heat a flat iron or a brick and wrap it in a towel and put it under the covers to warm the bed before we got in. I can remember waking up on a cold winter morning and seeing ice formed on the windows—the *inside* of the windows.

Another thing... Our doors had no locks on them. Nobody ever locked their doors back then.

We always had chickens for eggs and fried chicken, and they roamed free in our yard. Where chickens roam free, they leave droppings on the ground, and it was not the most pleasant thing to walk in the yard barefooted, like we always did in summer, and feel something squish between your toes.

Chances are you had stepped in a chicken *dab*. If Mother wanted to fry a chicken, she would send us boys to the backyard with a homemade *chicken catcher*. It was a long piece of heavy wire with a crook on the end. She'd tell us which pullet she wanted to cook, and we'd sneak up and hook the crook around the chicken's foot. She'd take it, wring its neck, and scald it in boiling water, and we'd pick the feathers off.

I still remember the smell of a chicken that had been dipped in hot water—an unpleasant odor.

Daddy bought us an *ice box* after we moved in. With no electricity, it was literally as the name implied—*ice* box. Once a week, a truck would leave Natchitoches and stop at country homes to deliver ice. My folks would order a 50-pound block of ice, and by the time it got from Natchitoches to Goldonna, it probably weighed 35 pounds.

I still remember the name of the ice man, Mr. Monk. He would use ice tongs to bring our block of ice into the house and put it in the box, and we had a way to keep our milk and such cool. *Sorta.*

On hot summer days, ice would be chipped off the block to put in our ice cream freezer where we took turns turning the crank to finally produce some of the best homemade ice cream ever. The only time Tom and I tasted ice water was during summer when we would crawl under the house to where the water dripped through a funnel to the ground below and catch the cold water on our tongues.

About the *path* referred to earlier... About 50 yards in the back of the house was our outdoor toilet. It wasn't bad to visit during summer but try to imagine having to go out there, pull your britches down, and do your business with temperatures below freezing. I don't think toilet paper had been invented back then, but we had no problem coming up with a substitute—an expired issue of Sears Roebuck catalog.

With no electricity, you couldn't save meat or vegetables without them spoiling. We always had a pig we would fatten up, and on a chilly fall morning, the pig would be slaughtered, cleaned, and cut into pieces—hams, shoulders, sausage, etc.

Next to our house was the *smoke house* where the meat was hung from rafters over a fire of hickory or oak that would smolder and produce smoke to permeate the meat and give it a wonderful aroma and flavor. After the meat was *cured*, we had a *meat box*—a big box with a hinged lid that sta̲ Mother and Daddy's bedroom.

The meat was packed down and covered with a type of ، that would preserve it for months. Want a ham or bacon? (to the meat box and whittle off what you needed.

I remember how good it tasted and smelled being cured. I don't ever remember it spoiling.

We always had a garden where we all worked planting, hoeing, and picking. Mother canned lots of vegetables to be used during winter. We would dig potatoes and place them under the house in a cool shady spot. The potatoes were sprinkled with lime and covered with hay to keep them from spoiling.

We didn't have the conveniences kids do today growing up, but nobody else in Goldonna had them either, and we never felt deprived. I wouldn't take anything for my upbringing in the country with fine Christian parents.

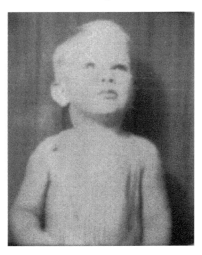

ₑd in
alt

₁y Mother:
ₑ "Mae" Meek Harris

My mother—we didn't call her Mom or Mama—was barely five feet tall, but for the three of us growing up as her kids, she was bigger than life.

She had the capacity to love deeply and was quick to defend her kids if there was a threat.

Once we lived in New Orleans while Daddy worked in the Delta shipyard during World War II. I was uprooted as a second grader in the tiny rural Goldonna school and placed into the highly urban McDonough 19 school in New Orleans.

It was frightening for me and not easy to adjust from being a country kid to one thrust into a culture of city kids of different nationalities. One particular family lived next door, and there was a daughter who was older than me, and she was a bully.

She picked on me on the way to school, and you could see something building up in my mother as she was ready to defend her second-grade son.

One time, my brother Tom and I obtained some sort of whistles and were sitting on the front steps blowing them. After a while, the bully girl came over to tell my mother that her dad was sleeping, and the whistle blowing was bothering him. Mother rose up like a mad wet hen, I'm sure with hands on hips and told the kid, "Go tell your daddy to put cotton in his ears."

Mother was the youngest of five surviving siblings. Seven or eight others were either still born or died at birth. They assumed my mother wouldn't make it, but she defied the odds and lived, indicating that she was born with a lot of grit and gristle.

Times were fairly hard on our family growing up as we didn't have a lot of luxuries, but as kids we didn't know it because Mother would make sure we had clothes to wear and food on the table. Regarding clothes, I remember wearing shirts she made from material she bought and particularly of wearing under shorts made from Acorn cow feed sacks. Sometimes the shorts had a figure of an acorn on the seat!

I learned about God from my mother. She made sure we were in Sunday School and church every time the doors were open. She sang in the choir, and I think taught Sunday School. She also ingrained in me a love for nature, songbirds in particular.

I can remember when she would hear an unfamiliar bird song and would reach for her well-worn bird book, and with her three kids in tow, she'd head out to locate the bird and determine its identity. She would also take us out at dusk to count stars and taught us to catch lightning bugs, put them in a jar, and later release them. I think my mother played a big part in me eventually becoming an outdoor writer.

My sister Linda provided the following information.

Mother was baby number 13 for her parents. The cemetery already held eight little graves in a row. The babies had been stillborn or died within a few weeks of birth. Today we know about blood's Rh factor, but in 1912, a tiny baby girl born eight

8

weeks premature at home and in the dead of winter was just another tombstone to be prepared.

Things looked so bleak, the midwife didn't tie the baby's umbilical cord. As a result, Mother nearly bled to death shortly after birth. Her parents, so accustomed to heartache, had not even chosen a name. The repeated losses hurt too much.

But the tiny baby survived the night, so the next morning the midwife named her Lemee—after the Lemee House on Front Street in Natchitoches. She wasn't given a middle name. It didn't seem necessary.

The old house was drafty, and December winds can blow cold in houses heated only by a fireplace. Our grandmother developed an infection and ran a high fever for several days. When the midwife offered to put the baby in a separate place, her mother declined and held the dreadfully small baby close.

Mother always said that her mother's fever probably saved her life and served as an incubator to keep her stabilized. At any rate, the unlikely little scrap survived to become the spoiled baby of two parents who had both been orphaned at an early age. Three older sisters doted on her, and an older brother showed his devotion by making her the target of teasing and pranks.

I don't know when she became a Christian. I just know that she did. She was raised to be a lady, a decent young woman. Her growing maxed out at 5 feet, 2 inches. She graduated from high school and longed to attend college, but no finances were available to make that dream come true.

Mother and Daddy—"Mae and Doc"—met after he got out of the Navy. I don't know the date. On their first date, he stole some sugar cane for her, then she cut her finger peeling it. Most of their dates were at play parties—house parties with music and dancing. Doc's brother got kicked out of the church for attending one. He must have gotten rowdy. Doc joined the other guys for a nip in the yard.

Mae was a premature and babied baby. Her folks didn't approve of him. He was persistent. They married at the preacher's house and spent their wedding night at her parent's house. The rooms had no ceiling. Mother said that she was safe—lol. There was a cat in the house who slept in the rafters, and before everyone went to sleep, Doc yelled, "Mr. Meek! Your cat's looking at me!" Everybody laughed.

Whatever attracted this sweet Christian girl from Readhimer to the rambunctious, unruly, unsaved, beer-drinking young man from Goldonna, no one has ever been able to explain. But she was. She cried and prayed and threatened to leave him time and again. He would straighten up time and again, and he was scared "Mae" meant what she said.

Two little boys were born within two years of each other. She kept praying. One day God came walking into Doc Harris's life, and her prayers were answered. Immediately, the drinking stopped, but the rambunctiousness never did. A daughter was added nine years later.

I remember Mother at the stove, in the garden, at the wringer washing machine on the back porch, and in the barn milking cows and birthing calves. I can still see her stopping whatever she was doing to hunt the bird making that strange call. She had spent most of her childhood in the company of Miss Caroline Dorman, so Mother knew every bird that was native to our homeplace and every one that was a migrant. She taught all three of us to recognize birdcalls and to be able to tell when a blue jay found a snake, when a cat was getting too close to the baby mockingbirds, and when the first whippoorwills and purple martins returned to our house and fields in the spring.

She also taught us to take care of folks who had less. Whether it was the elderly neighbors or missionaries on the foreign field, she did what she could to help. She was faithful to her church—teaching Sunday School, Vacation Bible School, working in WMU, cooking dinner for visiting preachers, and singing in the choir.

She died when she was still in her 60s—six years after burying her husband. All three of her children are Christians who serve the Lord in church, are married Christians, and all her grandchildren are Christians. Those who have married are married to Christians. Even her great-grandchildren who are of age have accepted the Lord.

Daddy put the fizz in our lives, but Mother was the rock. She anchored us all. Her unfailing faith and trust in God are why every Sunday morning there are folks in church in Goldonna, Ruston, Deridder, and Baton Rouge, Louisiana, as well as Dallas, Houston, and someplace in Missouri.

When you have faith the size of a mustard seed—when you're not much bigger than a mustard seed yourself—God has promised He will hear, and He will bless.

On Mamaw's front porch.

*Glynn and his two girls (Cathy left, Kayla right)
and Mamaw Mae.*

My Daddy:
Ernest "Doc" Harris

My dad. My memories of him growing up are positive ones.

Before I came along, they say that my dad was quite a rounder, but by the time I was born, he had become a Christian, and all I ever remember was a dad who was a good man. Dad had a sense of humor like few others I ever knew.

He could find humor just about anywhere—like the time he laid down for a nap when my girls were there, and they found

his false teeth on the bedside table biting down on a cigarette. He left them there for the girls to find.

For disciplining me, my brother or sister, he left that to our mother. I don't remember my dad ever taking a belt or switch to us since he was too softhearted. However, I so totally respected him for the man he was that, spanking or not, I didn't want to disappoint him.

When I was growing up, my dad worked for the Wildlife and Fisheries Department in predator control, better known as a *wolf trapper*. It was so exciting in the summer when Tom and I got to go with him to run his traps, maybe finding a wolf or bobcat.

My memories of growing up with a dad like Thomas Ernest "Doc" Harris still flood my mind today, and I realize just how fortunate I was to have had a daddy like him.

My sister Linda provided the following information.

Daddy was number thirteen out of 14 children. His dad married and had three boys and three girls. His mother married and had three girls. Their spouses died, and they met and married and had five of their own. He was next to last and came along in 1909. Thomas Ernest Harris. They named him for his dad's brother—T. H. Harris, the state Superintendent of Education.

They all moved to Goldonna from Jackson Parish when Daddy was about two years old—drawn by fox hunting of all things. Dr. William Golden, founder and namesake of Goldonna, lived here. Somehow, my grandfather was a fox-hunting buddy with him and wound up buying 80 acres of land for $100 and a mule. The descendants of William Austin Harris still live on that land. Five generations.

Ernest somehow was given the nickname of "Doc," and that's what he was known by all my life. Mother always called him Ernest though (sometimes with a squeal)—like the time he told her to go fix him and his brother some coffee. That feisty little lady told him that if he wanted coffee, he could fix it himself. He put her in the well, holding her hands, and listening to her squeal until she relented. Lots of laughing and lots of coffee. Lord, she loved that man.

But she threatened to leave him unless he gave up his drinking and got right with God. In fact, I'm not too sure that she hadn't left him for a while anyway. I have a letter dated August 22, 1938, addressed to her at her sister's house in Shreveport where he told her about accepting Christ after a night of sleeplessness and prayer.

He hit the ground running, eventually becoming a church member, a Sunday School teacher, a deacon, Sunday School superintendent, choir member, and song leader. He was the most entertaining daddy any kid could have.

My two older brothers probably never could recall Daddy not being in church. They all lived in New Orleans when he worked in the shipyards, building war ships during World War II. But the pine hills of north Louisiana called him home.

He made a living by running a sort of taxi service for people who didn't have cars, sold Watkins products door-to-door, worked for the highway department, and finally landed a job with the Louisiana Wildlife and Fisheries Department as a trapper. He learned the trade firsthand. By the time he retired, he was the Supervisor of Predator Control. I spent every summer riding with him to check his trap lines for nuisance varmints. I can still walk down a dirt road and *read* it like a newspaper as to track identification of who has passed through.

I don't know how many people he led to the Lord or encouraged them in their walk. Right up until his death, his church and church family took a high priority. He was a good friend, honest to a fault, a great daddy, but I bet he was a frustrating spouse to live with!

He never knew about the little boy in New England that was the result of an overnight shore leave when he was in the U.S. Navy as a 20-year-old. Long before he met my mother.

Life would have been quite different for all, I'm sure. Knowing Daddy the way I do, the little fellow would have grown up in Goldonna. But we will never know for sure. I just know that I sure did love him.

Papaw and his granddaughters, Cathy and Kayla.

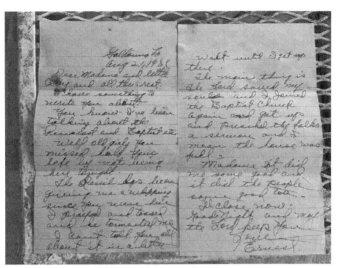

Papaw's Letter to Mamaw

17

My Grandparents

The Meeks

I have few memories of my grandparents on my mother's side. I vaguely remember seeing them and what they looked like.

Tom Meek was my mother's dad. I remember him as slightly built and bald. All the grandkids called him "Paw Meek." My grandmother, Edna Meek, was called "Maw Meek" by the grandkids. That's all I remember of them.

They're buried in Weaver Cemetery which is located along a side road between Readhimer and Creston.

The Harrises

I have some memories of my dad's parents because we lived next door to them in Goldonna. He was Papaw to us grandkids, and she was Grandmaw. I remember during summer Papaw had a big garden.

When watermelons got ripe, I can still remember him hollering "watermelon," from the back door to let us grandkids living on either side of him know he was about to cut a ripe watermelon. He had a scant amount of wispy white hair and always wore suspenders to hold up his britches.

Sadly, I was at his house the night he died. His daughter, my Aunt Vivian, was a schoolteacher. Another teacher, Louise Pullig, and Aunt Vivian boarded with Grandpaw and Grandmaw. I was having trouble with homework, probably math, and had gone next door for help when Grandmaw came into the room crying, telling us that Grandpaw had just died from a heart attack.

He was the only one of the Harris sons who was not a doctor or educator. He chose to farm while several of his brothers became doctors or teachers. His younger brother, T.H. Harris, was a long-time Superintendent of Education for Louisiana. They grew up around Homer in Claiborne Parish, and T.H. had a school named in his honor. The small village of Langston south of Homer has long been known as the Harris community.

My grandmaw was a little dark-haired lady, always wearing an apron as I recall. One of the main things I remember about her is her habit of dipping Garrett Snuff. It came in a brown bottle, and she transferred a portion to fill the small can she carried with her.

Every afternoon it was her habit to take a nap, and if it was warm enough, she would raise a window by her bed. She would take off her apron, which contained her ever present box of snuff, and hang it on the bedpost while she napped.

One day, my cousin Doug, who was a year younger than me, and I hatched a plan. Grandmaw made dipping snuff look like so much fun, so the two of us sneaked up to the open window, reached for the apron, and retrieved her box of snuff. Then we sneaked off to the peach orchard that grew next to the house to give the snuff a try. We were probably 10 or 12 years old.

Doug went first. He got a pinch of snuff and put it in his lower lip and then handed me the box. He was apparently overcome with the devil because when I raised the box to my mouth preparing to take a dip, Doug reached over and slapped the box, sending dry powdered snuff into my mouth, nose, and throat. I honestly thought I was going to suffocate.

He got a big kick out of that, but for sure I didn't. We returned the snuff box to her apron before she woke and without her knowing of our escapade.

Grandpaw and Grandmaw are buried next to each other in the Goldonna cemetery.

My Siblings

I grew up with one of each—a brother, Tom, who was two years younger, and a baby sister, Linda, who was 11 years younger.

When I was two years old, my baby brother, Tom, joined our household. My mother told me the story of something that happened shortly after he was born.

I was a curious two-year-old, and one day, while Tom was lying on the bed, I thought I'd teach my baby brother some stuff. Mother walked in and to her horror, saw that I had my newborn brother by the head with his little feet on the floor. and I allegedly commented, "My *wittle bruver* can't walk." She, of course, rescued the tiny baby, and I got a good scolding I would imagine.

Somehow, Tom survived the incident and from all accounts, suffered no long-lasting effects from having his little neck stretched!

Tom and I had two other *brothers*. Actually, they were our two first cousins, Doug and Sambo Harris, who lived on the next hill over, and we were always together doing stuff that little country cousins did like sneaking off before it was warm enough to go swimming in the creek or going bird hunting with our homemade sling shots.

Then there was little sister, Linda, who the whole family spoiled because she was the youngest and the only female.

Tom (left) holding Linda. Me (right) holding our cousin.

One of the most memorable things I can recall had to do when our mother had some rotten eggs she wanted Tom and me to dispose of. They were not chicken eggs. They were guinea eggs. We had a few guinea fowl mixed with our chickens.

The shells of guinea eggs are much harder to break than chicken eggs. Realizing this, Tom and I began playing *catch* with a rotten guinea egg, tossing it back and forth a little harder each time just being macho I suppose.

As our tosses grew harder, we didn't realize that our two-year-old little sister had wandered to where we were playing pitch and catch. I don't remember if it was me or Tom who made the last toss, but little Linda had toddled in between us without our noticing.

The rotten guinea egg struck our little sister upside the head, and the egg exploded. Rotten eggs smell awful, but rotten guinea eggs are even worse. She ran screaming to Mother who got her comforted and cleaned up before turning her attention to Tom and me. I don't remember, but if I had to guess, we got our behinds whipped and deservedly so.

Tom, Linda, and me.

Linda, my new brother, Paul, and me.

My Childhood Holiday Memories

Thanksgiving at our house was always something special, especially what my mother created in her kitchen. Two things that I recall sharply are her hen and dressing.

Not turkey and dressing—a fat hen and dressing.

I don't ever remember eating turkey when I was growing up. Another thing I remember her making was ambrosia. I recall orange and coconut in the dish and how good it was. Of course, there were pies and cakes that were outstanding. I don't remember anybody joining us for Thanksgiving. It was just us.

One thing I always did after we ate this great dinner was what I'd do that afternoon. No football games. I would take my shotgun or rifle and go to the woods behind the house and squirrel hunt. I don't remember ever getting any, but it was just a tradition I always did.

Overall, Thanksgiving was a day where we not only gave thanks for our blessings but for the tradition of what Mother had cooked and had on the table—and the squirrel hunt.

Christmas at my house growing up. Man, what special memories.

I think it all started with the trip our family took to the woods out back to find a Christmas tree. It was not easy to find one perfectly shaped. One side would look good, but the back side was skimpy because of growing next to a big tree.

No problem. Mother would just set the tree in the corner and turn the skimpy side to the wall.

Decorations were simple—red roping, icicles, a few colored balls. No lights for one simple reason—electricity had not made its way to Goldonna during the early days of my growing up.

Another favorite memory are the smells that came from my mama's kitchen—wood duck roasting in a cast iron pot, gravy dark and rich, cornbread dressing, a hen, not a turkey, roasting. We never had turkey growing up, but no problem, we were catching a chicken from the yard, wringing the neck, and scalding it.

Desserts? Oh my! Chocolate pie, pecan pie and my all-time favorite, applesauce cake. Even today, my wife Kay and my daughter Cathy, make me applesauce cake for Christmas. Just wouldn't be Christmas without it.

The night before Christmas, Tom and I would go over from our house on one hill to the next hill where our cousins, Doug and Sambo, lived. We'd build a big bon fire and shoot fireworks. I especially remember those big red two-inch firecrackers that could remove a finger if handled carelessly.

After fireworks, it was off to bed, but sleep was not easy to come by because I couldn't help thinking about what I might find under the tree the next morning. Tom and I would often wake up and jump out of bed long before daylight to see what was under the tree, and I was never disappointed.

We didn't get the fancy stuff kids get today but a BB gun, toy truck, hard candy, apple and orange, and maybe a board game.

My most memorable gift was when we were really small, and we each got a pedal car. Daddy had found them somewhere, maybe in somebody's garbage, but he brought them home, hammered out the dents and gave them a shiny coat of blue paint. I guarantee you no brand-new, store-bought pedal car would come close to providing the thrill we got when we saw those two blue cars under the tree.

Probably my favorite Christmas memory was when it came time to sit down for the noon meal Mother had prepared. Before we sat down, she prepared a tray with everything we were about to enjoy, and the whole family would walk through the pine thicket to the home of an old couple and share our food with them. Otherwise, they would not have had such a fine meal.

It taught me something that has stuck with me all my life, and that is about the joy of giving. What sticks out in my mind the most is the lesson it taught us kids as Mother and Daddy used the occasion to remind us about the greatest gift ever given when God sent his son Jesus Christ to Earth to show us how to live and then to die and take the penalty of our sins on Himself.

Through our faith in what He did, we have the promise of life everlasting in His presence when our days on Earth have ended.

Mother's Cookin'

For breakfast, we'd hop in the car and run to Mickie D's for a sausage biscuit.

Just kidding. McDonald's hadn't even been invented yet.

One thing I could always depend on for breakfast were biscuits. Mother made them homemade *every single morning*. I can still see her, apron on, standing over a big bowl where she kept her flour, pouring in buttermilk and lard, mixing it all with her hands, and pinching off egg-sized pieces of dough to put in the skillet for baking.

Some mornings, especially when it was cold, her oatmeal was really good. I especially liked that we had real cow cream to add to the hot oatmeal. After milking the cow, the milk was chilled overnight, and a layer of thick cream formed on the top. She would skim the cream off the top to put on the oatmeal. You talk about good!

We ate lots of vegetables for dinner and supper that we grew in our garden. We didn't call it lunch and dinner. Purple hull peas, sweet corn on the cob, potatoes, tomatoes, okra— all the good stuff, and Mother could convert them into great meals, especially when she made a fresh pone of cornbread.

Usually on Sundays we'd have fried chicken. Did we run by

KFC to pick up a box? *Nope*—just like McDonald's, it hadn't been invented yet. She would send Tom and me to the yard to catch a nice frier for Sunday dinner. She would cut it into pieces—I always loved the drumstick and wing—and fry it, and with it she made a pot of rice, homemade gravy, and, of course, a fresh pan of biscuits.

Desserts are my weakness, and Mother could really turn out some tasty stuff—chocolate pie, lemon icebox pie, banana pudding, coconut cake, yellow cake with chocolate icing. I loved them all. At Christmas, her signature dish was applesauce cake.

When I was a little bitty kid, I loved cookies and milk, and I have no idea how I started calling milk bookie, but I did. I can visit either of my daughters or granddaughters today, and at the end of meals, they make sure I get my *cookies and bookie.*

Another thing was what Mother packed us for school lunch in a brown paper bag. We always had some sort of beef or pork the grownups had slaughtered, hung in the smoke house and then salted down in the meat box. I could always find a piece of meat inside a biscuit to make a sandwich. It might be ham or bacon.

For dessert, I always looked forward to what she packed— a couple of biscuits and a small jar of ribbon cane syrup. In order to enjoy this treat, I'd poke a hole in a biscuit and pour syrup into the hole I'd created. There might have been syrup dripping off my chin, but oh my, that was so good!

The Adventures of Glynn, Tom, Doug, and Sambo

Boys need boys, especially country boys.

I was fortunate to grow up with three: my brother, Tom, and two first cousins, Doug and Sambo. We were stair-steps. I was the oldest, Doug was a year younger than me, Tom was a year younger than Doug, and Sambo a year younger than Tom. We lived on a hill that had earned the name, *Harris Hill*, and on the next hill within sight of our house is where our cousins lived.

Summertime meant no school and three months of country fun. We would always try to rush the arrival of warm weather. I can remember taking off shoes and how your tender toes felt when you first stepped onto grass that had just begun to turn green. As the summer wore on, the soles of feet that had been tender became like leather from going barefoot all summer, and that's what the four of us did.

The activities we typically did involved bird hunting and fishing. It pains me today to think about our bird hunting using homemade sling shots armed with small round rocks from the gravel road in front of our house. The only birds that were protected from our sling shots were the purple martins that nested in our bird boxes and orioles that nested in our trees. Every other species of bird was fair game, and that's sad.

Then there was swimming and fishing. We were fortunate to have a pond and a creek that ran through the woods behind our house. I'm not sure of the correct spelling of the creek, but phonetically, it was *Molly-Dough*.

There was a railroad track that separated the creek and the pond, and they simply named the pond Tank Pond. It had that name because at one time there was a big water tank sitting next to the pond where the steam locomotives would stop and fill their tanks. The four of us learned to swim in the *Tank Pond* before moving on across the tracks to the creek in the woods.

We would sometimes spend summer nights camping out on the bank of the creek while we were setting out hooks for catfish. We cut down small saplings to use for poles, and bait was earthworms. During the night, one of us would wake up and announce, "Let's go run the hooks."

One night, I was sound asleep when the call was made. I hopped up and started walking toward the creek. Tom had a stuttering problem, and he saw I was headed for the creek bank in the dark and tried to warn me, but his stuttering and sputtering didn't work. I stepped off the bank into the creek in the middle of the night, half asleep, but you can be sure I woke up in a hurry when I hit the water!

On another occasion, the four of us went swimming in the creek, and we had a little puppy along with us. I was paddling around in the water with the puppy when I felt a sharp pain behind my knee. I assumed one of the boys had sneaked up and pinched me, but I looked over and saw they were all up on the bank, but something had me by the leg. I reached down and pulled out a long black water snake, threw it aside, and scooted up the bank to survey the damage.

The three boys joined me to try and figure out what should be done. A snake had bitten me, so Doug thought it best to cut through the site and let the poison drain. About the time he whipped out his rusty old pocket knife, I noticed there were no fang marks, only a row of tooth marks, so I was in no danger of dying from a snake bite. I was relieved, but Doug was disappointed because he didn't get to use his first aid skills on my leg.

As adults, we married and grew apart, but some fifteen or so years ago, Doug came up with the idea of getting the four of us back together on his pond to catch fish, clean and cook them on the pond bank, and have the chance to remember the old days when we were growing up like brothers. It became an annual tradition where we got together like this for a day. Tom passed away seven or so years ago, but the remaining three Harris boys enjoyed what we called our *Cuz'n Fish Fest*. After years of enjoying it, it came to an end in 2023 when Doug passed away.

Goldonna

I have no idea what it's like to grow up *in* Goldonna because I didn't. I grew up a mile from town on a gravel road out in the country on Harris Hill. Since Goldonna was the closest town and it was where we went to school and church and bought groceries, I suppose you could say I grew up in the metropolis of Goldonna, a tiny village with a couple hundred population.

I have some special memories of that village. My first cousin, Jack Easley, owned one of only a couple of stores there. I don't ever remember seeing my mom and dad go to get something from the store and pay for it. Jack kept a running tab, and at the end of the month, Daddy would settle the bill.

I remember a big old oak tree in front of Jack's store that had a bench around it. I can remember seeing some of the town's old men sitting around talking and whittling. Everybody had a pocket knife.

The L&A railroad ran through Goldonna, and I can still remember lying in bed on a summer night and hearing the old steam engine huffing and puffing up the track and sometimes stopping for water at the Tank Pond behind our house.

The Goldonna Baptist Church was where we attended Sunday School, BYPU (Baptist Young People's Union), RAs (Royal Ambassadors), and VBS (Vacation Bible School) in the summer. It was at the church when I was in high school that I felt the need to accept Christ as my Savior and I did. I was baptized down on Saline Creek at the Old Landing swimming hole.

Goldonna High School was a two-story brick building that housed grades one through twelve. My first-grade teacher was Mrs. Jessie Quarles, and she gave me my first spanking I had in school. At recess I was running through the room and knocked off a little porcelain lamb of Mrs. Jessie's, and it broke. She bent my hand back and paddled it with a ruler, then made me sit at my desk with my head down. I eased my head up later to look around, and one girl in the room tattled on me. "Mrs. Jessie, Glynn's not crying!" So I put my head back down in a hurry and started sniffling a bit, just in case it was needed!

When I graduated from high school, I can say I graduated in the "Top Ten" in my class since there were only ten graduates! I graduated with Donel Trichell, Billy Eaves, Larue Lucky, and Marvin Weaver, and the girls were Luda Weaver, Eddie Jo Conley, Nelda Smothers, Bonnie Fae Kieffer, and Betty Jean Cloud.

Growing up in and around this tiny town has given me a deep appreciation for the experiences I had. I wouldn't trade it for anything.

Childhood Toys

When I was growing up, our toys were, for the most part, what we made them. A pocket full of marbles could entertain us for hours. We'd draw a circle in the sand, put our personal marbles inside the circle keeping out a favorite *shooter* marble. The objective was to take turns shooting our marble into those in the circle, trying to knock an opponent's marble outside the circle, which made that marble yours.

I remember a network of roads we made in the dirt underneath our house which was not on a slab but on elevated blocks. We would make roads, and although we seldom had toy cars, our grandma's empty brown snuff bottles were just right to push along the roads we made. On hot summer days it was cooler under the house.

Pretending we were cowboys meant that Tom, Doug, Sambo, and I would spend summer days shooting at imaginary outlaws. We had cap pistols, those little fake guns loaded with a roll of caps, which included a small bit of gun powder. Once you pulled the trigger, the hammer hit a small pocket of powder, there would be a *pop* sound. If we didn't have cap pistols, we cut a fork of a sapling and used it as a substitute.

Later on, we built slingshots by cutting a limb off a sapling where it branched into the shape of a *Y*. Then we took rubber inner tubes from abandoned car tires and cut the rubber into strips that we fastened to the two legs of the *Y*. Next, we took old discarded or worn-out shoes and used the tongue of the shoe as a pouch to hold a marble-sized round rock. Tying the pouch to the rubber bands, you could pull it back and propel a rock with some accuracy.

I'm ashamed to say that some of the objects of our sling shots were songbirds. We didn't know any better back then.

Chores

Growing up in the country was quite a bit different than growing up in a city.

Goldonna was a tiny town, and I grew up a mile from that little town. There was no Wal-Mart or Super One we could visit for groceries. We grew what we ate, and that had a lot to do with my chores growing up. In the garden one of my jobs during the growing season was to join my brother, mom, and dad in picking peas, pulling corn, digging potatoes, etc. Picking them meant corn shucking and pea shelling.

We had a milk cow for as long as I can remember growing up. By the time I got to high school, it was my job to milk the cow before school. I'd have my school clothes on, but I kept an old pair of pants in the cow barn I'd slip on to do the milking. The cow would be waiting for me to put feed in the trough, and she would begin to eat while I'd do the milking.

In my early years before electricity came to Goldonna, we had a wood stove for cooking and a wood-fired heater to keep us warm. It was my job, no matter if it was cold or raining, to "bring in some stove wood."

As much as I complained and whined about having to do chores, when I look back on it now, I can see what a blessing it was and how it helped mold me into who I am today.

Diseases of My Youth Unheard of Today

When I was growing up, it was not at all uncommon for kids to get diseases that are unheard of today. Scientists developed a vaccine, and widely administered it in 1971 which pretty well curtailed the diseases that kids my age were subject to.

Red measles was one. I remember when a measles epidemic began, and it seemed every kid in the area, including me, woke up with fever, a headache, and a rash. We had to stay away from other kids until the illness ran its course.

Another was one I well remember—mumps. The glands in your neck would swell and become sore, which was accompanied with pain, fever and general feeling sick.

Rubella was another—better known as German measles. I don't remember if I ever had that one, a nasty condition that included such symptoms as enlarged lymph nodes, a red rash, a headache, and runny nose.

Then there was whooping cough. It was somewhat comical to listen to a kid with whooping cough. The condition was correctly named because when you had it and coughed, it sounded like a raspy *whoop*. It made you sick with some of the same symptoms as the others, but the dead giveaway was the *whoop*.

Thankfully, the MMR vaccine administered to kids starting back in 1971 has made these childhood diseases I grew up with virtually non-existent.

There was another condition I had my share of—boils, or as we called them *risens*. I think they were really staph infections. I had several as a kid, and although they rarely made you sick, they created problems because the painful red pus-filled bumps could crop up just about anywhere on your body. Until it drained, you had to protect it from being bumped because it hurt like the dickens if you did.

I remember one time I had one on my bottom, and although we went about our daily activities as normal, we were careful not to bump it. While in a group of folks, an older fellow was joking around, and he swatted me on the rear with his hat. I didn't want to cry and complain, but what he did caused the boil to burst, and I don't remember anything ever hurting like that did.

Thankfully, I eventually outgrew all that bad stuff that attacked us as kids.

My Love Affair with the Guitar

My love for the guitar began early in life, probably before I realized I had such interest in music.

Looking back, it was a God thing because He gifted me with a special *ear* for music, not just loving to listen to good music but having something inside that let me know if a note or chord I was hearing was on or off.

I didn't grow up listening to opera or pop music. It was all country for me. I'd sit around our old battery-operated radio and tune in to the Grand Ole Opry and the Louisiana Hayride to listen to their music, especially how the guitars sounded.

One day when I was maybe in junior high, we were visiting a cousin and one of 'em had an old beat-up guitar. They didn't want it and asked me if I did, so I took it home. There were two problems.

I had never played a guitar, and this one was so old and beat up the neck was warped with strings an inch off the fret board. My daddy took a length of wire and attached it to both ends of the guitar. Then he found a green stout stick and used it to wind the wire tight enough to straighten the neck out enough to play, tying the stick off so it would remain in place. Try to picture playing a guitar with a stick and tense wire against your stomach. Had it come loose, I would have likely lost a belly button!

Daddy showed me the three chords he knew–G, C, and D–and I tried for a while on the old guitar, but it was no use. Daddy saw how much I wanted to learn so even though money was tight, he found a guitar in the Sears Roebuck catalog and ordered it for me. I felt guilty about him having to spend $14.95 on a guitar, but he wanted me to have it. I waited for the mail every day from the day it was ordered until it finally came. I would sit around the radio with my guitar and try to mimic what I was hearing on KWKH, my favorite Shreveport country radio station. I remember practicing until my fingers were sore and tender, but I loved it so much I gritted my teeth and kept at it.

I learned to pick fairly well, strumming chords and being able to change from chord to chord easily. My daddy was so proud that I was learning to play, and after a couple of years, about the time I finished high school, he ordered me a little solid body yellow Silvertone electric guitar and small amp from Sears. He said he would order it on one condition—that I would never start smoking. I assured him I wouldn't.

One day I was at college and a group of us pickers were in a dorm room playing when Daddy walked in unannounced. I introduced him to the guys, and he made the announcement that he had bought me that fancy yellow guitar so I would not start smoking. All the guys began glancing at me because there on the amp sat an ash tray with a lit cigarette that nobody was claiming. I think my daddy knew he had been had. It's one thing I really hated—being dishonest with my dad who bought me two guitars and loved to hear me play.

At college, I was introduced to some really good pickers, including one in particular, Sonny Montgomery, who was amazing. He also played lead guitar in the Demonaires, the college dance band. When he graduated, he recommended me to take his spot, and I got the job even though I couldn't read a lick of music. I just listened to the music and learned the chords.

I have continued playing with different groups of pickers through the years, and just before Kay and I married, I played for a couple of years with the Wildwood Express, a well-known local band that played in Ruston's Dixie Theater every Saturday night.

As I have grown older, there are two things that help keep me from acting so old—being able to write outdoor columns every week for the past 50-plus years and having to be creative to do this...and being able to play my guitar with a group of guys that have met and played together every Thursday night for at least 10 years.

To me, the thing God has blessed me with is being able to really hear music. Not just pretty songs but in knowing when it's right and knowing where "stuff" is on my guitar, being able to think a few notes ahead to hit the right "stuff" at the right time. What a blessing I have been given!

A History of Hunting

My life as a hunter began when I was not much older than a toddler. My daddy would take me along to introduce me to what hunting was all about long before I actually started toting a gun and hunting myself. When I was first allowed to carry a gun—a single shot .22 rifle—I would go with daddy, and he'd instruct me about what to watch for when a squirrel was feeding or moving about a tree.

My introduction to deer hunting took place in Claiborne Parish when we lived in Homer. I had always enjoyed squirrel hunting and became good friends with James White who worked with the school board. James had a squirrel dog, and we had lots of fun together following that dog. Then when deer season opened, I'd lose my squirrel hunting partner because James loved to deer hunt more than he loved squirrel hunting.

One day I was squirrel hunting alone when I heard a hound barking back in the woods, and as it got closer, I was mad because I figured my squirrel hunting had been messed up. I saw something move and a big buck stepped out of the woods and looked in my direction before taking off. Hmm, I thought. Maybe there is something to this deer hunting because it was exciting seeing that buck.

I told James about my experience, and he suggested that I come along with him next time he went deer hunting. I told him I'd like to, but I didn't have a deer rifle, I only had my shotgun. No problem, he said. Buy some buckshot, and that will work just fine, so I did.

The date of my first deer hunt was November 24, 1967. We were hunting near Summerfield with a friend, Bill Bailey, who had a pack of hounds he used to chase deer. James, his three sons, and I strung out along a pipeline out from Summerfield waiting until Bill turned his hounds out.

Before long, I could hear the hounds coming, and they were getting closer. Suddenly, a buck burst from the woods, and instead of running across, he turned down the pipeline and ran right in front of where I was sitting, probably 20 yards away. I raised my gun and fired. The buck was still up, so I fired again and then a third time before the deer fell. The last shot I fired took one side of his rack off.

An eight-point taken on Two Creeks Hunting Club on November 28, 2015, is the last buck I've killed.

When James came to congratulate me, he had a question: why did I shoot him three times? Because he was still running. James's comment still rings in my ear and brings a smile. "Son," he said, "you gotta give him time to fall!" I was able to find the half of the rack I shot off, glue it together and that 10-point rack now hangs in my office.

The biggest one I ever killed was an eight-point that measured near 140 inches, killed on Calhoun Farms Hunting Club one mile from my house on December 23, 1998, during a big ice storm.

There is another species I was reluctant to start hunting—wild turkeys. Springtime for me meant fishing time because the bream were bedded, big bass were in the shallows getting ready to spawn, and I couldn't wait for each spring to go fishing. Then an outdoor writer friend, John Phillips, called me with an offer to come to Alabama for a turkey hunt. I thanked him kindly and declined the invitation because of my love for spring fishing.

Then he dangled a carrot in front of me, things like free airfare, a guide, a new shotgun, set of camo clothing, turkey calls, etc. It didn't take me long to decide the bream and bass could wait a few weeks, so I agreed. I was introduced to my guide who met me at the airport, a fellow whose name belied what body type he was. "Skinny" Hallmark weighed close to 300 pounds and proved to be not only a good guide but a special friend, and I went back to Alabama several years in a row at my own expense to hunt with him.

On that first hunt, we stayed in Skinny's hunting cabin far back in the woods around Rockford, Alabama. The little cabin had no electricity, no water, and no bathroom. In other words, really rustic but comfortable. On that first morning, I followed Skinny down an old woods road in the dark. We stopped, and he started mimicking an owl. An owl? I thought we were hunting turkeys! However, his owl call triggered the first gobble of a wild turkey I had ever heard.

He silently pointed to a big tree and whispered for me to get my camo face mask on and sit by that tree with my gun on my knee. Then he backed up a few feet behind me and started calling on his turkey calls. That's when I heard him gobble, and it made my heart flutter just a bit. In a minute or so I saw something coming through the woods. It looked like a white softball levitating above a mass of something dark.

As my eyes adjusted, I realized I was looking at my first strutting gobbler, and my heart really took off. I was afraid the gobbler could hear it. I did as Skinny had instructed me, the turkey stuck his head up, I shot, and he dropped.

I had just killed my very first wild turkey gobbler, and I was immediately hooked and made myself a vow that I may run off all the turkeys in the woods, but this was something I was going to learn to do myself.

I have been fortunate over the years to have taken 41 gobblers, and I did it all around the country from Alabama to Texas and Florida to South Dakota where I have been blessed to have qualified for the Wild Turkey Grand Slam, getting at least one of all four subspecies living in the U.S.—the Eastern, Rio Grande, Merriam's, and Osceola (Florida). What a blessing getting to chase gobblers has been!

Hog Killing Time

Back when I was growing up out in the country, when you wanted ham, pork chops, or a side of bacon, you didn't run to the supermarket to get it, for at least two reasons. One, there was no such thing as a supermarket in Goldonna back then. Second, why try to find your pork at a store when you had it right there in your house, in the meat box, in your parents' bedroom?

There are some necessary steps, however, in moving a live hog you've been feeding in the pig pen to the meat box. That involves hog killing day.

First, your daddy and the adults who would be involved in hog killing had to select the day for the event. It usually took place in the fall, and it had to be on a cold day to prevent spoilage of the meat.

The hog selected for the event might have been somewhat of a pet as us kids fed and even petted them there in the pen where they were *fattened* up. On hog killing day, the hog was put down by a single shot from Daddy's .22 rifle. Next, the hog had to be *scalded* to remove the coarse hair on the body. That was accomplished by having, several hours earlier, a big black pot filled with water and heated by building a fire under it.

The hog was dunked into the hot water which loosened the hair making it easy to scrape off. The finished product was a naked pig devoid of any body hair.

Then the pig was *gutted*, sort of like field dressing a deer. Various organs such as heart and liver were set aside to be sliced up and cooked later. Then there were the intestines. We simply called them *hog guts*. They were saved to be converted into *chitlins*—city folks call them *chitterlings*. I still have a vivid memory of watching Grandma Harris, my daddy's mom, clean a tub of hog guts, stripping them of whatever was inside them. It was not a pretty sight, but one I remember all these years later.

After they were cleaned, the hog intestines were cut into sections, boiled until tender and then fried to make crispy snacks. I could never develop a taste for them, personally. However, I did love the intestines when they were converted into sausage casings.

Once the meat was removed from the pig—the hams, shoulders, sides of bacon, sausage, etc., the meat was hung to cure in the smoke house in our yard. A slow-burning, smoldering fire of a savory wood like hickory or walnut produced lots of smoke which was necessary to cure the meat that hung over the fire.

The curing event took several days, and I can still remember the wonderful aroma coming from our old smokehouse.

Then came the meat box. A special kind of curing salt was used to preserve the meat since we didn't have electricity and thus no deep freezer. The meat would be completely covered, top and bottom with the salt, and six months later when my mother wanted a ham or shoulder to cook, she would dig into the meat box, find the meat she wanted, brush the salt away, and cook it like we do a ham now.

Memories of hog killing day are special to me still today.

Childhood Friends

My childhood friends growing up consisted mostly of my brother and two cousins—the Harris boys.

Our favorite time of year was spring when we could shed our shoes and go barefoot. We would fish down on Molideau Creek behind the house catching perch and bass, but our most special trips were at night when we would set out hooks for the mudcats in the creek. We would sometimes spend the night on the creek bank with no worry about mosquitos or snakes. It was just plain old country fun.

I had some other friends at school and would sometimes spend the night at their homes. One was a classmate named Donel Trichell who lived way down in the swamp. Donel eventually married another classmate, Luda Mae Weaver. Then there was LaRue Lucky, a classmate who lived up the road from us. We would sometimes ride bikes together around the *Loop*, a dirt road that started up the road from our house and looped back to the town.

Other friends were Roy and G.W. Conley, and we often played music together.

This photo below is of the entire senior class at Goldonna High School in 1955: (left to right) standing, Luda Weaver,

Donel Trichell, Eddie Jo Conley, Billy Eaves, Nelda Smothers, Bonnie Keiffer, Marvin Weaver, Betty Jean Cloud, Larue Lucky, and Juanita Houck and sitting is yours truly.

Seasons

———◆———

Preparing for season changes today is a far cry from the days when I grew up. When it begins to get warm now, we flip on the A/C. When winter weather comes, a flip of the switch turns the system to heat, and in both cases, we have comfort. Not so when I was growing up.

Today it would be unheard of to live in a house with no air conditioning or heating, but for us, we didn't have it for one basic reason—electricity had not made its way to Goldonna yet. Once we got electricity, Daddy bought a couple of fans and we thought we were living in luxury!

When the weather warmed, every window in the house was thrown open to let any breeze that happened to be blowing cool the house. The funeral home hand-held fans moved the air around a bit, and for us kids, there was always the creek where we could swim to cool off.

I remember nights during summer when the heat of the day that lingered into night was so strong it was hard to sleep. The window by the bed Tom and I shared was open, but it faced the gravel road in front of the house. Any car that passed left a cloud of red dust hanging in the air that made its way through our window, and you could smell it. So we not only had heat, we had dust to contend with. Other ways we stayed cool in summer was making homemade ice cream using an old hand-cranked freezer. Seems like it took forever for the ice cream to be made, but there was nothing better than a bowl of hand-turned ice cream.

Wintertime was also a challenge. There was a wood heater in the living room that we gathered around to stay warm when the weather was really cold. I didn't look forward to bedtime because of having to crawl into a bed that was ice cold. However, my mother had a solution—she would heat up a couple of flat irons she used to iron our clothes, wrap them in a towel and put them under the covers to help warm the bed. She would pile on quilts until it was hard to turn over from the weight of the covers. We slept in our *long johns* and that helped keep us warm too.

Today when I think back on the change of seasons when I grew up, I doubt I could handle now what we had to go through. But back then, it's just what we did. We made the best of what we had.

Bamboozled by a Bobcat, Scared Witless by Wolves

I always idolized my daddy in his job, especially the one he retired from, that of being a wolf trapper.

First though, I have a faint memory when I was just a little kid of riding with him as he drove around his route selling and delivering Watkins Products. I remember one time we stopped at a house where an old friend of his lived, and as

always, Daddy liked to sit around and chew the fat. He had a knack for that.

On this occasion, Daddy took out his plug of Browns Mule chewing tobacco–that was before the loose-leaf kind like Beech Nut came along–cut off a chew and handed the plug to the other guy to cut himself one.

It must have looked really good to me because I asked Daddy if I could have some. Seizing the opportunity to make a point with me and forever kill my taste for tobacco, he cut me off a chew and sat back to watch and see if I'd turn green. I didn't. I loved it and have had a love affair with the *devil's leaf* ever since. I tried smoking for several years, eventually changing to a pipe until my wife's complaints about tobacco odor penetrating her drapes, so I quit. However, today an occasional pinch of chewing tobacco suits me just fine.

When my daddy worked for Wildlife and Fisheries as a predator control agent, aka wolf trapper, it was always a thrill to go with him to run his traps. Once on a hot dry summer day, I was with him when he approached where he had set a trap and it was gone. Something had gotten in it, and the ground was dry so there was no track and no way to know what had gotten in the trap.

His traps had an eight-foot chain which was attached to a *drag hook*. When something got in the trap, it would take off dragging the hook behind and become entangled in brush after going a short distance. He told me to go search one way while he went another.

As I was walking slowly along looking for any sign of what was in the trap, I noticed a rotten log with the bark disturbed like something had gone over it. Growing beside the log was a sapling, and as I approached the log to about six feet, I happened to look up.

Something caught my eye, and there in the sapling with a trap on its foot was a big bobcat.

I'll never forget the look on that cat's face. In its eyes, it was as if it was saying, "Go ahead, buster. Take two more steps, and I'm on your head." I jumped back and yelled for my daddy.

That about scared me to death. Talk about a hair-raising experience!

On another occasion, Tom and I were permitted to spend a week with Daddy as he trapped wolves in Madison Parish. Daddy and the caretaker of the hunting lodge where we stayed had located a wolf den back in the swamp, and they hatched a plan to get the wolves.

Daddy had taught me how to howl like a wolf, and the plan was for Tom and me to stay at the Jeep while Daddy and the caretaker sneaked in halfway from the Jeep to the den, and for me to howl after ten minutes. He left me his watch.

The plan was as the wolves responded to my howling and headed our way, they'd be ready with their shotguns to ambush them. I howled after ten minutes and got an immediate response from wolves at the den.

I waited to hear shots but after a couple of minutes, I decided to howl again.

The wolves answered, and suddenly here they came, three of them looking for the *howler*. They had somehow slipped past the two with the shotguns.

Daddy kept a pistol under the seat in the Jeep, so Tom

sneaked out, got it, and fired, not to hit a wolf but to scare them and keep them from eating two mighty frightened little boys. The wolves skedaddled out of there, and when Daddy and the guy showed up, they found two little boys white as sheets and shaking!

Moon-shine in
the Church House

I grew up in a small country church, Goldonna Baptist Church. My mom and dad never failed to have Tom, Linda, and me there anytime the church doors were open.

That included, in addition to Sunday School and worship service, BYPU (Baptist Young People's Union) on Sunday nights and on Wednesday nights, R.A.s (Royal Ambassadors). There were lots of scripture memorization, Bible drills, Bible School in summer, etc., and looking back on all that, I'm thankful I was exposed to church, the Bible, and the plan of salvation early in life.

Sometimes things would happen in church that caused you to take your mind off the preaching and singing though. For instance, one Sunday morning, my cousin Doug and I were sitting together, and our moms were seated together across the aisle and slightly behind us. It just so happened that one of the pillars of the church was seated on the pew in front of Doug and me. It was a warm Sunday morning, and the elderly gentleman seemed to be especially cool and comfortable.

Our moms saw it first—why he was so cool. His seersucker

pants that I'm sure he had worn for years had become quite thread bare, and as he stood and leaned over for a hymnal, his britches split from his waist all the way down. One of our moms said to the other, "Keep your eye on Glynn and Doug to see if they see what we see"—which was a bare bottom.

The elderly gentleman was not a fan of wearing underwear.

I can't remember which of us saw it first and nudged the other, but we were standing two feet from this distinguished gentleman's bare bottom shining through the split in his pants. There was no way we could control our giggling and shaking, we were so tickled. Our moms said later they knew exactly when we spotted the "moon," we were shaking to keep from laughing out loud and disrupting the service.

That was one scene that has stuck in my mind ever since, and anytime Doug and I are together today, we laugh all over again at that spectacle we observed one warm Sunday morning. In addition to learning about and accepting Jesus as our Savior, that time Doug and I watched the "moon shine" in the pew in front of us, was a life-time memory maker.

The "Pitture" Show

Going to the "pitture" show was a rarity if you grew up in Goldonna back when I did. There were a couple of theaters in Winnfield where we seldom got to go. In fact, I don't remember a single time I went, although I guess I may have.

What I *DO* remember is a company that would periodically set up a tent in Goldonna and show movies. I remember sitting on a bench in that tent and watching The Lone Ranger, Hopalong Cassidy, and Lash LaRue in western shoot 'em up cowboy movies.

When I was in high school, there was a drive-in movie in Winnfield, and I can remember Daddy letting me borrow the family car and taking Mercille, my girlfriend, to the drive-in show. We didn't have television, so I couldn't watch movies on TV.

On another matter, I remember when the first TV was bought in Goldonna. John Dupree, father of my brother-in-law, Roy, had one, and men and boys in the community would come at Mr. Dupree's invitation to watch the *Friday Night Fights*, aka boxing matches, on his TV.

If you got there late, you had to stand on the porch and look through the window at the snowy, dim black-and-white picture. Those old TVs had a picture tube about 12 inches across while the tube sat in a box as big as a refrigerator. But we thought we were really getting to see something special.

Which reminds me of the first color television we saw. We would take our two little girls downtown in Winnfield where there was a store that had a color TV. They kept it on at night for the public to watch through the window. We would take the girls, sit in the car, and watch *Mitch Miller* on TV in living color!

Grandpa Harris, me, and a wolf.

Dogs I Have Known and Loved

When you grew up in the country as I did, dogs were as much a part of life as the chickens that pecked around your yard, the milk cow chewing a cud in the pasture, and the pig in the pen waiting for the weather to get cool enough to be converted into hams, bacon, and sausage.

Some of the dogs I remember living in and around the Harris household back then were Tippy, Rusty, Boots, and Bitsy. Maybe there were others, but time has erased their memories.

After leaving home, graduating from college, and starting a family of my own, dogs continued to be a part of my life.

The first one I recall was Jody, a little half Cocker Spaniel. Instead of being a pure-blooded Cocker, the mom apparently met up with a mongrel down the street. Before his pedigree was learned, we even had his tail docked like his mom. Even though he turned out not to be a full-fledged Cocker, we loved that little guy and were devastated when he was out chasing a girlfriend and crossed the road ahead of a car, and the Buick won.

Then there was Bambi, a little doe-colored Chihuahua. She was a tiny little bundle we loved until her old age meant we had to have her put to sleep. I've had to do that with others that followed, but Bambi was the first and it hurt the most.

Trixie was next, and she came to us in a most unusual manner. Kay, my wife, was working downtown when a lady came by the office where Kay worked holding a bedraggled little white pup she found wandering the street, a dog she couldn't keep. Kay brought it home, and we took her to the vet to get her cleaned up and learned she was a full-blooded poodle about two years old.

She came to us with no name, and we tried calling her by several names to see if she would respond. When we said *Trixie*, she perked up so we assumed her former owner had named her that or something similar. We put a notice in the paper but never got a response, so Trixie enjoyed a full life with us until we had to do for her what we did for Bambi.

Then there was Rufus. We started scanning the ad section of the paper for puppies available for adoption and located one, a Papillion, that caught our attention. It was love at first sight, and we brought little Rufus home with us where he enjoyed a charmed life for over 16 years. It was one of the saddest days of our lives when we had to have the little fellow, who had grown deaf, nearly blind, and had developed serious health issues, put to sleep. Kay and I decided that maybe our lives with dogs as companions was over. It hurt too much to part with those little fellows we had loved so much.

A lot changed in the year and a half since we lost Rufus. We finally concluded that after memories of Bambi, Trixie, and Rufus had faded, our home was missing something we had enjoyed for years. We decided we needed to get another pup to fill the void and began praying for divine direction to be sure we were making the right decision.

It was almost by accident that we discovered a lady with a pregnant female Yorkie who would soon be having puppies available for adoption. The sire was a long-haired Chihuahua and the dame a registered Yorkie, so we put our name on the list.

Easter Sunday afternoon in 2022, we brought our little eight-week-old Chorkie home, all two pounds of her, and gave her the name Coco, which seemed just right for her. It feels good and right to be back in the puppy business again.

Becoming a Writer

My career as a writer started somewhere inside me early on as I loved to read all those hunting and fishing stories in the outdoors magazines. It was something inborn, and if you had asked me back then what I wanted to ultimately do, I doubt it would have been to become a writer. That didn't come until later.

My high school English teacher was my aunt, Lillian Montgomery, and I think she may have seen something in me to indicate that maybe I could write. She was tough on me, probably tougher than others in class who were not her nephew. I found out that what I really liked to do, what gave me a bit of a thrill, was imagining a hunting or fishing trip and trying my hand at writing about it.

I thought I was getting pretty good when I got up the nerve to write a fictitious story about a deer hunt. I named it *Big Burn Buck* about me outwitting a huge buck where there had been a fire that burned much of the area.

I was so proud of my efforts that I got up the nerve to send my story to one of the most famous outdoor writers I knew, the late Grits Gresham, who lived in Natchitoches and who was a friend of my dad. I asked him in which of the big-time

magazines he thought I could get my wonderful story placed—
Outdoor Life, Field and Stream, Sports Afield.

I was all excited the day I got a letter from Grits, and I couldn't wait to open it and learn where my career would take me. Grits was easy on me and in a nice tactful way told me something like "I think you might have trouble selling your article," but he then gave me some advice about learning to write which he compared with trying out for the Saints football team. Every team member got there because of more than just ability but hard, disciplined work.

I was disappointed when reality hit that I was a long way from being a writer. After moving to the town of Homer, I got up the nerve to walk into the office of the local newspaper, The Guardian Journal, and asked if they were interested in hiring a *hunting and fishing* writer. I didn't even know the term was outdoor writer. The lady in charge told me no, and I was strangely relieved because had she said yes, I'd have had to start writing.

Six months later, I was in the newspaper office, and she approached me and asked if I was still interested in writing for the paper. This time I was ready, and on September 1, 1972, my first column appeared in The Guardian Journal. I was too embarrassed to put my name on the article, so I called myself *Uncle Zeke from Beaver Creek*. I still have some of those early columns, and they were awful, but I learned to write by having to write every week.

Later, I joined some professional outdoor writer groups, Outdoor Writers Association of America and Southeastern Outdoor Press Association as well as the Louisiana Outdoor Writers Association. Joining these groups, I became friends with some of the country's best-known writers who were extremely helpful to me in getting my feet wet in the profession. Over the years, I have been fortunate and blessed to receive over 60 Excellence in Craft awards from these organizations for my writing.

That first column appeared over 50 years ago. Since then, my writing has expanded to national magazines, including the "Big Three" I asked Grits Gresham about. My outdoors coverage expanded to outdoors radio in 1983, and today, I still broadcast four radio programs every week plus write my weekly columns that appear in newspapers and parish journals across north and central Louisiana.

God gave me a gift I didn't realize I had early on but with the passage of years, I have come to see just how richly He has blessed me in helping me finally evolve into what He intended for me. It is very special to be making a living doing something I dearly love.

Major News Stories
in my Lifetime

There have been a few major news stories I have lived through over the course of my life.

The first one that comes to mind, although my memory of it is dim because I was seven years old, was the end of World War II. We lived in New Orleans while my daddy worked at the Delta Shipyard. I vaguely remember the family going down to Canal Street to join the enormous crowd in celebration of the end of the war.

The parade and bands playing brought a time of relief and joy. I didn't know what it was all about, but I remember a good feeling that everybody was celebrating.

Another one I vividly remember was when I was at work with the Department of Public Welfare in Natchitoches, and we got the news that President John F. Kennedy had been assassinated. I remember the feeling of not only sadness but deep concern as to how anyone could kill our President. It was a somber time, especially when television coverage showed the whole horrific happening.

Also while at work, someone had a television on to report

the launch of the Challenger spacecraft, and we were all stunned when it exploded, taking with it the lives of the astronauts aboard.

Still later, I had retired from my job with the state and had settled in my job as an outdoor writer. I was on the phone in my office interviewing a biologist for a story I was writing when the biologist abruptly stopped talking and asked if I had my TV on.

I turned it on in my office in time to watch a plane fly into one of the twin towers in New York City. The date of that event, September 11, 2001, has become synonymous with global terror and how it affected not only our country but the world.

Other major events that didn't make national news but were the highlights of my life were on July 24, 1960, and November 9, 1964, when my two precious daughters were born.

Stories Told About Me

I have had a few stories passed down about me from my mother.

When I was a little bitty sprite, crawling around on the floor of our rural home, I did what any other baby would likely do—look for things that seemed tasty to a baby. I didn't hesitate to pop it in my toothless little mouth.

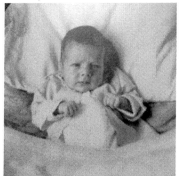

My mother tells about one time while I was crawling around the floor, she noticed I seemed to be enjoying something I had in my mouth, chewing and munching. She inspected to see what it was. We had a house cat named Gray Boy—that we found out when it had kittens it should have been named Gray *GIRL*!

The cat had apparently finished a meal of something it had found and had discarded the remainder that I was munching on. Mother ran her finger in my mouth and extracted the object I was obviously enjoying. Know what it was?

The head of a mouse that Gray Boy no longer wanted.

Today, I'd have probably been taken to the doctor to get decontaminated, but other than Mother becoming nauseated, I suffered no adverse consequences from chewing on the head of a mouse.

On another occasion while I was still little, a family of birds—chimney swifts—had taken up residence in our chimney, constructing nests and rearing their young. Apparently one of the little swifts had tumbled from the nest, and while I was crawling along the floor, I found the little bird, and when Mother came to see what I was doing, I had extracted a leg from the hapless little chimney swift and was munching on a tiny drumstick!

My Education

Let me start with my education path that began in first grade in Goldonna. Mrs. Jessie Quarles was my teacher, and except for the time I broke her little ceramic lamb and got a spanking, it was a good experience including falling in love with Betty Jean Cloud. I smiled at her as sweetly as I knew how with an expression that is forever memorialized in my first-grade school photo (see below). I tried the pose on Betty Jean, and she responded by sticking her tongue out at me. She assumed I was making a face at her!

In second grade, we moved to New Orleans for a few months for my daddy's job at the Delta Shipyard. It was quite a shock leaving the quiet little country setting at Goldonna to start school in New Orleans. The school they assigned me to was McDonough 19, which was the first school in Louisiana to later be integrated.

We moved back to Goldonna and finished our schooling. After high school, I enrolled as a freshman at Northwestern State in Natchitoches. I remember the first test I took the summer I enrolled was in math, and when I got my grade, I had a score I had never heard of before or since. I made an F+!

My college years were fun—too much fun actually—because my grades were nothing to brag about. I was introduced to beer and enjoyed it too much, and I'm glad I gave it up after I graduated. I began making music with some guys in the dorm and was asked to play guitar for the college dance band, the Demonnaires, which I did for two years. I graduated with a bachelor's degree in business education, which prepared me for my first job, teaching business subjects for a year at Shongaloo High School.

After my year of teaching and a couple other sales job, I

landed a job with the Department of Public Welfare, and after two years, I applied for and was granted leave to pursue a graduate degree in Social Work from Louisiana State University. The experience went well, and there was a highlight that year when my youngest daughter, Kayla, was born at Baton Rouge General Hospital.

During this time, we lived in married student apartments, and another memorable experience happened when Hurricane Hilda took a direct shot at Baton Rouge. I remember watching out the window of our second-story apartment as the 100 mph winds hit. Quite an experience!

Courtin'

It was at school where I fell in love...several times. My first girlfriend experience took place, of all places, in the first grade.

I was sweet on Betty Jean, and when picture taking day came to school I had a plan to really win her heart. When I stepped in front of the camera, I produced a sweet little shy smile I was sure would win her heart. Later I tried the smile on for her, and she stuck her tongue out at me, accusing me of making faces at her.

Donel Trichel also had his eye on Betty Jean, and one time I remember he and I both buying a bag of penny candy. I'd give Betty Jean a piece, then Donel would give her a piece, I'd give her another piece and on and on.

It didn't work. She wasn't interested in us, only our candy! And we made Betty Jean sick with all the candy.

One other memory had to do with me picking cotton for S.E. Bedgood. I ate dinner at their house, and since I was sort of sweet on their daughter, I sat next to her. While cutting a piece of meat, my finger slipped, and I spilled gravy everywhere. Needless to say, she was not impressed with me.

Near the end of my high school years, I had a bit of a crush on Betty Jean's sister. I was a senior, and she was a freshman. My dad let me borrow the family vehicle, a baby blue Kaiser, and we'd go to the picture show in Winnfield and such. We courted until I finished high school and moved off to college, and we went our separate ways.

The Initiation

When I was attending college at Northwestern in Natchitoches, I was invited to join a fraternity, Phi Kappa Nu, one affiliated only with Northwestern, not a national one. I felt privileged to be asked to be a part of this group, most of whom were friends. Then came the day of initiation, and by the end of the day, I felt betrayed that their main goal was to see if they could kill me with the stuff they put me and the other pledges through.

First, we had to fashion a paddle. Every member had one, and this seemed special until I learned it could be used to administer some serious pops to the rear end by those already members. We had to parade around campus all day with a crazy hat and sign around our necks.

One of the contests we had to do was a race. A fairly steep hill ran from the gate at the entrance to the college to the field house at the top of the hill. We had to race up the hill, but in a very non-conventional way. We were given a piece of chalk and were forced to push the chalk all the way up the hill—with our nose! Nobody made it although we tried, but we soon ran out of skin on our noses. If you don't think that will remove nose skin, I suggest you try it.

Another thing they put us through had to do with a pencil attached to a string sticking a few inches out of the collar of your shirt. We were required to get autographs from girls with them using the pencil. The string attached to the pencil was so short, tugging was required to reach the paper. Use your imagination as to where the other end of the string was attached!

The night of the initiation was straight from the pits of Hades. We were blindfolded and forced to wade across creeks, having to do all sorts of things the older members required. A bottle of pure honey was poured down our pants followed by a cup of cornmeal. Try walking around all night with that!

When the night ended with a ceremony where we officially became members, our blindfolds came off, and we were told we could go back to the dorm. We didn't know which way to go because they had marched us around blindfolded all night.

Somebody figured it out, and we came out of the woods and made it back to our dorm, stripping off clothes as we ran. The most miserable night I ever spent—ever! But at least, I was an official member of Phi Kappa Nu fraternity!

Scary Moments

Growing up in Goldonna, things were basically good, and looking back on my growing up days, most I can remember came with good feelings. But not all. My mother was maybe five feet tall, but when we did something we knew we shouldn't do, she grew at least another foot especially when she reached over and broke a skinny little limb from the hedge that grew next to the porch.

When she did that, I knew I was in for a whipping that would sting like the dickens and make you have second thoughts about how to behave. Between the time she broke off the limb and applied it to my rear end was a particularly scary time.

Another time when I was scared to the point I thought I may not survive was when my daddy took me squirrel hunting and left me alone for the first time. He sat me on a log with my little .22 rifle and told me to sit still and watch for squirrels in the hickories in front of me.

He said he was going to walk just a little way down to the creek and hunt there and assured me I'd be safe and to just sit and wait until he came back. So there I sat, looking for squirrels.

The hour was getting late, and I started having a little concern that grew with each time I noticed the sun sinking lower. As the sun set and dusk began settling in, I was more than concerned. I was flat out scared, and I remember thinking that Daddy had forgotten about me and had gone home without me.

I could see myself getting eaten by a bear, wolf, or tiger, or just sit and die on that log in the dark alone. Then I heard a noise, something stepping on leaves in front of me, and I got ready to be eaten alive until I looked up and the one making that noise was my daddy.

Never have I been more happy to see him.

The Worst Christmas

Christmas 1992 was one I'll long remember—and I have the scars as a constant reminder. Cell phones had just come on the market, and my sweet wife surprised me with one for Christmas that year. When I opened the package, it thrilled me to find a new *bag phone*. While Kay was preparing our Christmas dinner, I decided I'd give the new phone a try, so I got in my truck, plugged the phone in, and was excited to see it light up, ready for use.

I had told Kay to expect a call from me as I backed my truck up and eased onto the road. Instead of stopping, I thought it best to make my call as I eased onto the road. I started dialing and realized I had dialed wrong. I was trying to figure out how to delete the number and insert the right one as I slipped the truck into second gear and crawled down the road.

When I noticed my truck appeared to lean to the left, I interrupted my dialing. I looked up to see I was heading for the steep embankment some 20 yards from my driveway. I could tell this was not good, so I cut the steering wheel hard to the right to get back on the road. It was too late.

I was too far down the embankment, and when I turned the steering wheel, my truck went rolling over one and a half times landing on its side in the ditch at the bottom of the embankment. On the trip down, as the truck was turning over, I had a machete behind the seat, and I recall it flying around the cab and barely missing me.

However, the steering wheel didn't miss me. It slammed into my mouth, relieving me of several teeth and doing serious damage to my lips.

When the truck stopped rolling, it was lying on its side. I was able to get the door open, crawl out, and walk back to the house 50 yards away. When Kay saw me walking in, she was in shock, thinking a deer hunter had shot me because there was blood streaming from my mouth. She got me in the car and took me to the emergency room where I momentarily blacked out from shock. They kept me overnight.

Two days after the accident, my sister, Linda, and her young son, Ben, came to check on me to be sure I was going to be alright. As they left, Ben handed me a note to read as they drove away. Here's what Ben's note said:

Uncle Glynn got a phone for his car.
Would it work? Which button? How far?
So, he went for a spin.
Did an end over end.
Now he has a new phone but no car!

Places I've Been,
Sights I've Seen

Growing up in Goldonna, rural and outback as you can get, about the most exciting thing I ever did or witnessed was a visit with schoolmates to the Carey Salt Mine near Winnfield. I remember our descent into the underground cavern and how cool and peaceful it was and how unusual it was to have an actual salt mine this close to home.

Another spectacle I witnessed as a high school senior was our senior trip. The beach? The mountains?

Nope...we loaded up on Homer Graham's yellow school bus for a trip to the big city of Shreveport to attend the Louisiana Hayride. Was a fancy restaurant in the plans?

Nope again...our mothers had fried up a bunch of chicken and fixings, and we picnicked at Ford Park on Cross Lake before heading to the municipal auditorium to see the stars we'd heard on the radio perform.

What a memorable night it was, especially during the *Beat the Band* segment when members of the audience were selected to come on stage and guess a song the band was playing. Classmate Donel Trichell was selected. He guessed the tune correctly and was awarded a prize by the sponsor of that segment—a five-pound bag of Martha White flour.

When Kay and I married, the world opened up for this *stay-at-home* country boy. As a travel agent, she was the recipient of several *fam* trips with all expenses paid for some fantastic vacation sites. On many of these trips, I could accompany her, and it was *country come to town* for me.

First off for our honeymoon, we got on a flight to Miami, where we boarded a Royal Caribbean cruise ship for visits to Grand Cayman, Montego Bay, Jamaica, and Cozumel, Mexico. As special as these visits were, we were just getting started. The cruise ship itself featured an all-you-can-eat buffet all day long every day, and as a result, I probably gained ten pounds.

I tried dishes I had only heard of and even though I'd rather have peas and cornbread, trying escargot and caviar was something I had to experience.

On another *fam* trip with Kay, we visited Puerto Vallarta, Mexico, where a couple of young guys who operated a charter boat took me for my first try at deep sea fishing.

Yet another cruise out of New Orleans took us to Key West and a couple of other Caribbean islands.

My daughters had married career U.S. Navy guys who were stationed literally all over the world. Being married to a travel agent allowed me to visit them in such places as Hawaii, Spain, and Scotland. Stateside, I got to visit them literally from coast to coast from San Diego, CA to Groton, CT.

My membership in the Southeastern Outdoor Press

Association took me to annual conferences in, as you might have guessed, the southeast. From Florida and South Carolina, North Carolina and Virginia, to Georgia, Alabama, Tennessee, Arkansas, and Mississippi, I made them all.

Let's not forget the trips I made once turkey hunting became my obsession. Besides hunting here at home, I have hunted turkeys in Florida, Texas, Connecticut, South Dakota, Alabama, and Mississippi.

One of the most fascinating trips Kay and I took was to England on our way to visit Kayla and Keith in Scotland. We toured Stratford-upon-Avon, the home of William Shakespeare, and in London, Westminster Abbey and Buckingham Palace. The flag flying over the palace gave evidence that Queen Elizabeth was there at home, possibly taking a nap or sipping afternoon tea.

I'm content here at home now, but memories of those special experiences around the globe often occupy my most cherished thoughts.

My Memories as a Father

I can't tell you my most favorite memory as a father. There are so many, but I'll start with my first one. On July 24, 1960, Dr. Grover Baum at Martin Hospital in Winnfield announced I was a daddy. At 23-years-old, when I first saw my Cathy, that little pink bundle of baby girl, I can't say for sure, but I'll bet some tears coursed down my cheek.

I remember a few months later when we lived in Mansfield, and I heard her laugh for the first time. I remember when she got ready to enter first grade in Homer, she wanted to walk into school on her first day by herself. When I let her out of my truck and watched her walk a few steps and then stop

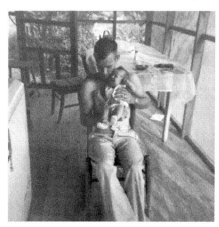

when she saw all the other kids, I wanted to get her and bring her home because I didn't think I was ready to let her be a first grader, wanting her to still be my little girl like she'd been the past six years.

When I was a graduate student at LSU, I became a dad to my second little girl, Kayla, who was born at Baton Rouge General Hospital on November 9, 1964. I remember problems of finding the right formula for her. We finally found one, and once when we were on our way to north Louisiana from Baton Rouge to show our baby girl off to grandparents, we stopped in a little town because it was time for her bottle, and we needed it to be warmed.

I stopped at a café, took her bottle in, and asked the not-too-bright worker there if she could warm my baby's bottle. She said she'd be glad to, but I was horrified when I watched the woman pour the formula from the bottle into a beat-up old pan and stick it on the stove to heat. I stopped her, but it was too late.

The bottle of formula was ruined, but thankfully we had another, and I don't remember, but I assume we let her have the bottle without it being warmed!

My two girls have been a blessing to me through the years, winding up marrying two of my favorite guys in the whole world, two devout Christian men. Cathy married Bill, and Kayla married Keith. The two couples have presented me with seven precious grandchildren and six great-grandchildren.

When Kay and I married, I got another bonus daughter, Melissa. She was just shy of ten years old when we married.

Melissa, too, has been a blessing. Married to another fine man in Ross, and they have produced three more grandchildren I love.

To me, being a daddy to these three has helped make me into the person I am. I am so thankful for the opportunity to fill this role. My prayer is that I will always have their respect and love.

My Memories as a Grandfather

One of the greatest privileges of my life has been to be a grandfather to a bunch of special young'uns. It all started with my first grandchild, Haley Beth, first born of my daughter and son-in-law, Kayla and Keith Johnson.

The first time I ever saw her was an experience in itself. Her parents were living in Hawaii where Keith was stationed with the U.S. Navy, and they flew home during the winter for a visit and to show off their first born. It just so happened that north Louisiana was experiencing an ice storm when they landed in Shreveport and were settled in at my daughter Cathy's home.

I had to risk the problems ice could cause because I wanted to get to see and hold my little granddaughter. Melissa and I risked the trip, and we made it fine. I got to see and hold and kiss my little Haley Beth.

Later in the afternoon, we planned to drive back to Ruston because the roads had thawed enough, but we lingered a bit too long and when we left, the roads starting freezing again. Long story short, we had to turn around halfway home because 18-wheelers were stuck along I-20 and we couldn't get through, so I was able to turn around and head back to Cathy's where we spent the night and got to get a little more Haley Beth sugar before finally being able to make it back to Ruston the next day.

Another Haley Beth memory took place in Connecticut when I was there attending my daughter's wedding to Bill Icenogle. After the ceremony, we wanted to see the fall foliage New England is known for, so Kayla, Keith, Haley, and I headed north for the two to three-hour drive to Vermont. Haley was a toddler at the time.

My wife, Kay, had sent Haley a toy make-up kit, and somewhere along the trip, the kit got misplaced, and the little lady was *not* happy. We made it to Vermont but had about five minutes to look at leaves because Haley was wailing. She had lost her *nake-up*. We heard that all the way back to Connecticut.

There was a similar not-too-pleasant event that took place with Cathy and her daughters, Callie and Catelyn. I had driven to their home near Memphis for a visit—Bill was stationed there with the U.S. Navy—with the plan to take Cathy and the girls to meet Cathy's mom in Jackson. Catelyn, who has blossomed into a sweet, pleasant young lady, was anything but that on our trip. She wailed and cried the whole way during the longest feeling trip I ever had in a car with a squalling young'un!

When they were older, it was such a fun thing to take Callie and Cate and also Hannah and JoJo to Roy's pond to fish. My job was not to fish but to keep hooks baited and take fish off hooks, which wore me out, but I wouldn't take anything for the experience.

Max and I had a special relationship as he was growing up. He was my little hunting and fishing partner, and it thrilled me to learn he had a musical touch and learned to play the guitar along with me. That was so much fun getting to pick and grin with my grandson.

In 1998, Keith was stationed on the island of Diego Garcia, and Kayla and their four were living in Ruston during the year he was deployed. It was such a pleasure for me to go over every morning to visit and go to the store for what they needed, which was always the "Three B's"—bookie (milk), bread, and booty covers.

The twins were two years old, and one of the most memorable things I remember about Hannah was when they would come to our house for Sunday dinner. Hannah would walk in and announce to Kay, *"KK, I not hungry. I want ice ceam."*

I would have to say that one highlight of my life has been being Papaw to a bunch of special grandchildren. With both Bill and Keith in the Navy and stationed around the globe, I got to travel to places I would never have visited. I got to meet grandson Billy in Spain, see Haley in Hawaii, and Haley and Max in Scotland.

After I married Kay, I inherited Melissa and love the three little girls she and Ross have produced. Olivia, Sophie, and Ila Grace are all super special to me, especially since they know me by the name *Papaw*.

I Never Had a Son

When I married and started a family, as a lover of all things outdoors, I secretly hoped I'd become father to a little boy who I could watch follow in my footsteps learning to hunt and fish. It didn't happen.

As much as I wanted a boy, there is no way on God's green Earth I could have been happier than watching my daughters do what little girls all pink and frilly do—Barbie Dolls, Betsy Wetsy, Donny Osmond, piano recitals—as I watched them grow up to become beautiful and special young ladies.

But I never had a son.

Cathy and Kayla both wanted to please their outdoorsy dad, and although they gave it a good effort, Cathy even fighting a gag reflex as I coaxed her into hanging onto the hind legs of a squirrel I was skinning, it just wasn't to be. I needed them to have a brother.

But I never had a son.

Later in my life, I married Kay, and she brought into our marriage a 10-year-old daughter. Again, no boys entered my life. Melissa tried, learning to love some of the outdoorsy things I loved like feeding and identifying songbirds.

But I never had a son.

Somewhere along the way, a 13-year-old kid found his way into my life. David was his name. He was first cousin to my daughters, and he spent several summers with us and even attended Ruston High School for a time. I finally had a boy with which to invest my love for the outdoors.

What a thrill it was to watch David following in my footsteps in the outdoors. I was with him when he shot his first squirrel. He and I high fived when he downed his first

deer. I showed him where to cast his lure when he hooked and landed his first bass.

He buddied up with a kid his age who introduced him to even more outdoors stuff. That young man, Keith Johnson, is my son-in-law, who is married to my Kayla.

Time passed, and David grew up and married and became a dad to two youngsters, a son and a daughter. We kept in touch, but our man-boy experiences became fewer and farther between.

A few years ago, a painful sensation behind David's eye became bothersome, and when he finally had a doctor check it, he found cancer that had spread and was making its slow but certain and inoperable path to David's brain, eye, face, and throat. Doctors told him he had maybe a couple of years to live.

Last year, David and I rekindled our special relationship that involved our mutual interest in the outdoors. Confined to his apartment in Hot Springs Village, Arkansas, he mounted a trail camera out back to take advantage of the wooded lot behind his apartment.

Spreading corn in clear view of his camera, deer were attracted to the corn, and for more than a year, he sent me images of bucks with no antlers, then bucks sprouting new antlers and ultimately bucks with sets of hardened antlers repeating the process again this spring.

The last deer photos he sent me were dated May 21, 2022, and after commenting on the photo, David added, "I'm having to take tons of pain meds and can hardly swallow. AJ (his son) is coming back this afternoon, and Kristi (his daughter) will be here Friday. I can't do much for myself."

Four days later, on May 25, David was gone.

He had assured me he already made peace with his Maker and expressed his upcoming death in the way only the die-hard LSU fan he was might do.

"It's Gods call now. He's the Umpire Crew Chief, and I'm ready when he calls. Like LSU baseball players at the start of the game, when the Umpire calls, I will come running, my heart full of joy!"

No, I never had a son, but I had David, and that's good enough for me.

Wisdom for the
Younger Generations

I have led a charmed life. Sure, there have been not-so-charmed times, but for the most part, I'm so very blessed.

Looking back over these 85-plus years, here are a few things that have worked for me, things I'd like to suggest that those who follow me might find a nugget of help.

Follow your dream. When I was a school kid in Goldonna, I developed a love for picking up pencil and paper and writing something—anything. I'd look at what I'd written and thought it was pretty good. Looking back today on some of my early writings, they weren't pretty good—they were pretty bad. However, just doing something I loved to do had merit because it eventually led to me becoming a published writer.

I didn't have the full picture at the time of what writing would ultimately mean to me. Looking back on it now, I can see God's hand steering me in that direction by opening doors and making me willing to take chances and take the bull by the horns to be assertive and not just sit by, want something and hope it would happen. Sometimes you just gotta make it happen.

No matter what, you must give God first place in your life. It took me years for that fact to really settle in because, especially when I was younger, like in college, I did what I wanted to do. Deep down, though, I had this feeling that as a Christian, that wasn't the way to go. I was so immature, and thankfully, through the years, I overcame that and realized God could direct my life a whole lot better than I could. And He has.

Be kind. It does my heart good to know that I have been able to interact with some who needed to see a smile or hear a friendly voice. One example is I try to show that I care for young people working at fast-food places. Admittedly, I can sometimes get annoyed when my words are met with stone silence or an air of indifference. I have to work on that because maybe that sullen person who doesn't respond positively may have issues I know nothing about.

I hope some of these suggestions can give my kids, my grandkids, and great-grandkids something to think about as they plod through this trip we call life.

Awards

I have been asked to talk about some of the writing awards I have received. First off, every single one of the 60-plus I have won has been special to me. The first is probably the one that is most special to me because it came totally unexpected. My dad had recently passed away, and I wrote an article about what he meant to me over the course of my life.

A short time earlier, I had joined outdoor writer organizations and noticed in a newsletter from the Southeastern Outdoor Press Association (SEOPA) that they were sponsoring a contest for writers, so I thought what the heck. I'll send that column in and see what would happen.

Several weeks later, I was sitting in my office where I was working as director of the Lincoln Parish Department of Public Assistance when a package was delivered to me. I opened it, and to my total surprise, I found a certificate saying I had won *runner-up* in the newspaper category for my story on my dad. That was in 1976, and the certificate still hangs on the wall of my office.

One special award that came as a total surprise was a few years ago when attending the annual conference of the Louisiana Outdoor Writers Association. I was called to the front to receive an award they have only given out a few times. It was the Arthur Van Pelt Lifetime Achievement Award the organization bestowed on this shocked and very thankful fellow.

Another was one where I was included in a group of north Louisiana athletes for my writing over the years—the Sports Legends of North Louisiana award. Then lastly, I was selected for membership in the Louisiana Chapter of Legends of the Outdoors Hall of Fame.

I have been an active outdoor writer for 50-plus years since September 21, 1972. Just getting to share my stories and columns with folks is a reward in and of itself. To be singled out for special awards is, as they say, just *icing on the cake.*

My Testimony

My Christian walk began when I was a tiny tot because my parents always had me in church. We were there Sunday morning, Sunday night and Wednesday night. There was Sunday School, BYPU, RAs, and VBS in summer. There would be revivals every summer that would last usually at least a week, sometimes longer.

One summer when I was maybe 10 or 12, our RA group attended a summer camp. At the conclusion of the camp, the camp pastor preached an evangelistic sermon. I was sitting next to my cousin, Doug. When the invitation was given, I don't remember if I punched Doug in the ribs or he did me, but I remember one of us saying, "I'll go, if you will." We agreed, walked down the aisle, and shook the preacher's hand. When we got home, our mothers were so proud that Doug and I were now Christians.

Time rocked on, and when I was about 16 or so, our young pastor, Rev. Danny Blake, preached a sermon that really hit me. I realized that although my name was now on the church role, the thing Doug and I did at RA camp didn't mean a thing. I was seriously under conviction that I needed to be saved, and when the invitation was given, I was super nervous, but I knew what I had to do. I walked down the aisle, took Bro. Danny's hand, and told him, "I joined the church and was baptized, but I wasn't saved, but now I want to be saved." He led me in a prayer where I gave my heart to Jesus, and I knew then and there this time I got it right. I confessed my sins, asked Jesus to save me, and knew immediately that I was saved.

I was baptized again on Saline Creek at the Old Landing where baptisms were held. I started having concern for Doug and wondered if he had the same experience as me. Later, Doug did as I had done, accepted Christ and became a leader in his church.

I have had periods of feeling very close to the Lord, other times feeling I had drifted away, but today, I know in my heart as much as I know anything at all, that I'm His and He is mine. As I grow older and closer to the time when I'll meet Him face-to-face, I have no doubts about where I'll spend eternity.

I remember when I was having my coronary artery bypass surgery, after I woke up, I remember so clearly that during the process, having had a thought in my mind of Psalm 23, the part about "yea though I walk through the valley of death, I will fear no evil for though art with me."

Another time while I was recovering, I was going for a walk at Lincoln Parish Park and became troubled at not knowing what it would be like when my time to depart this Earth came. The words of an old hymn I hadn't heard or thought of in years came into my mind—there is no doubt that God was answering my concern.

That old hymn has the line, "I won't have to cross Jordan alone, Jesus died all my sins to atone. In the darkness I see,

He'll be waiting for me. I won't have to cross Jordan alone." Immediately, I had my answer. I'm His, and I don't have to worry about what will happen when my time comes. All I can say is to quote comedian Jerry Clower, "Ain't God good?"

Favorite Verses and Songs

I have been asked to mention my favorite Bible verses and hymns. It's easy to think of the one verse that has guided my life and the one that was the motivating factor in my deciding to write this book.

I found a quotation somewhere and have it taped to my wall that has served as my motto and the driving force.

"If God has given you some special work to do that frightens you, it's your responsibility to jump at it. It's up to the Lord to see you through. As you faithfully do your part, He will do his part."

The verse of Scripture that nails this thought down is Proverbs 3:5-6.

"Trust in the Lord with all your heart, and lean not on your own understanding; In all your ways acknowledge Him, and He shall direct your paths."

I suppose I'm a traditionalist when it comes to naming my favorite hymns. I love the ones I grew up with, the ones that still speak to me and in a sense, feed my soul with inspired words that mean so much to me.

Some of my favorites are...

The Old Rugged Cross

Rock of Ages

Amazing Grace

How Great Thou Art

Songs I love at Christmas...

Silent Night

Joy to the World

O Come All Ye Faithful

O Little Town of Bethlehem

I would be remiss if I failed to mention a verse and a hymn that have been alluded to earlier in this book. Psalm 23 will always be special, and the hymn, "I Won't Have to Cross Jordan Alone," occupies a niche in my memory that will never be erased.

My Career

After graduating from college, I was offered my first job as a college graduate. I received an offer teaching in the field where my college training had led me, to teach business at a Shongaloo High School, a small school in Webster Parish.

For the first few months, we lived in an apartment in Haynesville, ten miles from Shongaloo. Then a house became available across the road from the school, and we rented it for the rest of that school year.

The nine months of teaching solidified my enjoyment of working with people. I enjoyed it, but dang near starved to death because of such a low salary. Although I wasn't contracted to return to the school for a second year, I developed a love for the kids I taught, and even today, over 60 years later, I occasionally run across a student I taught at Shongaloo.

Since my teaching days were apparently over, I started looking for another job. My search led me to the West Brothers Department Store in Natchitoches. They hired me to be the assistant manager of the branch store in Mansfield.

To be honest, working from early to late six days a week was not enjoyable, especially as I watched my shotgun and fishing rod gather dust in the corner from disuse. I began looking for another job. The manager of the store learned that I was looking elsewhere, so they unceremoniously fired me, and the search was on again.

I learned of an opening in Winnfield for an insurance agent with Metropolitan Life Insurance, so I applied and got the job. As much as I disliked working at the department store, I disliked having to sell insurance more. The idea of having to sell to make any money was just not up my alley. I wondered if I would be happy at *any* job.

I have always had an interest in weather and there was a time when I thought I wanted to be a meteorologist. I even wrote a letter asking how I could get into that business to the head weatherman at a Shreveport TV station. His name was B.P. Hughes. He never answered and so my quest to be a weatherman never materialized, although I love to keep up with weather today.

Word of an opening in Natchitoches to work at the employment office reached me, a state job that required a civil service test. I took and passed the test. Then I learned before I got certified, the job had already been filled.

However, that same civil service test also qualified me for a job with the state's Department of Public Welfare, and they had an opening in Natchitoches. I interviewed with the parish director, Joe Stewart, who hired me and thus began my 30-year career as a social worker.

I was visiting and taking applications for public assistance for needy folks. It was a job that I came to really enjoy because I was getting to interact with people, and that seemed to be my calling.

After two years in Natchitoches, I applied to LSU for a graduate degree in Social Work and got accepted. After receiving my graduate degree, I was offered a job in Winnfield as a Case Supervisor where I worked for a year until an opening became available for a Parish Director in Claiborne Parish.

I took the job in Homer, and while working there, the opportunity for me to do what I really love came along. I began my *second* career as an outdoor writer and started writing outdoor columns for newspapers, something I have done now for over 50 years, something I hope to be doing for the rest of my life.

For eight years, I worked in Homer, eventually transferring to the same position in Lincoln Parish where, except for a brief stint in Jackson Parish, I retired with 30 years of service with the Louisiana Department of Public Welfare.

My Most Important Person

It is a tough assignment, naming the most important people in my life. I have been blessed by crossing paths with and becoming involved with a number of people who have meant so much to me.

If I had to name the one person who has contributed the most to the person I have become, I would have to name a lady, Kay Lynn Baldwin Harris, my beloved wife of 39 years.

Here's why I chose her. She is a serious Christian who is close to God, and she and I have grown together in our Christian walk. Another thing about her is the way she has accepted my daughters and grandchildren as her own, and I have done the same for her daughter and grandchildren. We have the perfect *blended* family, and I give her much of the credit for that.

During my career as a writer, she has been the one who has encouraged me the most, and I would have probably given all that up had she not believed in me to the extent she has.

Kay Lynn has not only been a wonderful wife, but a trusted Christian friend and confidant I can share anything with. I love her dearly, and there is no doubt that she loves me the same.

The Simple Life

In this book, I have been sharing events about my life from my 85-plus years on God's good Earth. I began life on March 29, 1937, as the oldest child of my mother and daddy. Obviously, I remember little about being a baby. Looking back on what life was like for our family when I came into the world, things were far different than they are today.

We didn't get electricity for the first several years of my life. I remember doing homework by the light of a kerosene lamp. Mother was a great cook, and she did it using a wood stove. You built a fire out of wood from the woodpile out back to heat it up. A wood heater furnished heat for winter. Nights in winter could be brutal.

Summers could be brutal too with no air conditioners or fans. Windows were opened to catch whatever breeze might drift in, but otherwise, trying to sleep on a hot summer night was not fun. Dust was something I'll always remember.

Folks today might think we had it bad back then, but if we did, we didn't know it because everybody else lived like we did. When we finally got electricity and could have a well with a pump that brought water to the house, we thought we were really living. No longer would we have to wait for the iceman,

Mr. Monk, to arrive from Natchitoches once a week and place a 50-pound block of ice in the ice box to keep food from spoiling.

I could go on about hog killing time in fall and winter, how the meat was cured by hanging on rafters in the smoke house over a smoldering fire and once cured and stored under a heavy wrapping of curing salt. How good that fresh cured and seasoned pork smelled.

I have seen a lot of changes over the course of my life from a simple upbringing to today when anything you want is there at the flip of a switch or touch of a button. Although I would hate to go back to those days, I wouldn't take anything for having the experience of the simple life those days afforded.

My Legacy

What a blessing it has been for me to be a dad to two daughters, Cathy and Kayla, and a *bonus* daughter, Melissa. As I think back over the years that I have been a dad, and later a grandfather, and still later a great-grandfather, not only have I been richly blessed, but I feel a deep sense of responsibility to leave my children, grandchildren, and great-grandchildren a legacy that will hopefully inspire them to be the best they can be.

I grew up in simple surroundings without all the trappings kids enjoy today, but in my mind, I never missed a thing because I had two parents who guided, taught, and disciplined me to be the best I could be.

This is what I'd like those of mine that follow me to hang onto—find something you love to do, your calling. Even if it takes a long time, make it happen. I didn't know back then that I was to become a writer or a skilled guitar player, but there was something in my soul that directed me toward those without me even knowing it.

Looking back on it now, I can see God's hand on my life as a youngster guiding and directing me to writing and music.

My number one prayer, my passion, is that all of those

mentioned who follow me will put their trust and faith in God and claim the salvation that can only be granted by trusting in Jesus Christ.

Following is an e-Thought I recently wrote that, in my view, sums it up. God bless each of you who read this story of my life. I love you all.

FOR UNTO US A CHILD IS BORN

Some of the happiest, most meaningful moments of my life have been when I held my newborn daughters in my arms and marveled at what God had permitted me to experience. The soft tender sweetness and innocence I beheld in the face of Cathy, then later Kayla, touched my heart in ways few other experiences have—until my grandchildren came along.

Oh my, to be privileged to once again know the joy and happiness of my daughters' children added a dimension that was right up there with when I first saw Cathy and Kayla.

As I have become older, yet another layer has been added to my love for my offspring and their offspring. My oldest granddaughter, Haley, is a mother of four. Recently, they were here for a visit from their home in Missouri. The distance between their home and mine means I'm fortunate if I get to see my great-grandchildren once a year, but I felt something similar to the feeling I had when I first held Cathy and Kayla.

How must Mary and Joseph have felt when they beheld their newborn son to realize they were holding a gift from God that the prophet Isaiah had forecast from centuries earlier?

In Isaiah 9:6, the prophet writes:

For unto us a child is born, unto us a son is given: and the government shall be upon his shoulder: and his name shall be called Wonderful, Counsellor, The mighty God, The everlasting Father, The Prince of Peace.

My children, grandchildren, and great-grandchildren have provided me a legacy that will live long after I'm gone. Because I have placed my faith in the Prince of Peace, the legacy promised by Isaiah will be mine throughout eternity.

Author's Note & Acknowledgements

My sister, Linda Dupree, does not shy away from the willingness to give a swift and to-the-point opinion whether or not one is requested.

At the outset of this project, I mentioned to her my plan to produce a book of my upbringing and stories about my life. She studied me over; the wrinkles, thinning hair and senior citizen status gave her a one-word response that hastened my quest to get the book done quickly. Her response?

"*Hurry!*" My children have been urging me to get my story down in print so they could have it to share with their children and their children's children. I have finally decided to jump into the project head-first starting with my first memories of growing up in the country alongside a red dirt gravel road.

What has amazed me is that the stark difference between conditions back then and conditions today are, in a manner, so different yet the same basic thread that connects who I was as a youngster growing up in a different time and place to echo who I am today.

I want to give a sincere word of thanks to a host of friends in the media who took me under their wings when as a fledgling writer I was accepted as a member of the Louisiana Outdoor Writers Association and the Southeastern Outdoor Press Association. I can't put a price tag on their acceptance of me and the guidance they offered.

I have to give a genuine tip of the hat to my editor, Morgan Tarpley Smith. Without her expertise and guidance each step of the way, this project would have never gotten off the ground. I would also like to thank one of the most thorough proofreaders, Carole Lehr Johnson, who is not only a dear friend but who volunteered her time to make the manuscript pop. Thanks to both you special ladies.

I want to give special acknowledgement to my sister, Linda, whose one-word response got me off high-center and got me started writing. A special word of thanks goes to my two daughters, Cathy and Kayla, and my "bonus" daughter, Melissa, not only for their love but for their belief in me in producing my life story.

Finally, my wife, Kay Lynn, has been my best encourager and critic. Her love for me and her desire to see this product reach fruition has been the number one thing that has kept me going. Her positive response when approving of something I write or her not shying away from something I write that she questions has overall made me a better writer.

I dedicated this book to someone who passed away decades ago, my high school English teacher, my aunt, Lillian Montgomery, who was extra tough on me and the work I produced because she saw something that indicated my potential as a writer. I just thought she was being mean. I would like nothing more than to be able to hand her the first copy of this book, hug her neck, and thank her for getting me on this path to doing something I dearly love, and that's sitting down and stringing together words that folks like to read.

About the Author

Glynn Harris is an award-winning outdoor writer, columnist, broadcaster and photographer based out of north Louisiana. Over the past four decades, his articles have been published in dozens of publications including Field and Stream, Outdoor Life, BassMaster, Louisiana Sportsman, Mid-South Hunting and Fishing News, Arkansas Wildlife, newspapers state-wide and more.

In 2021, he was inducted into the Louisiana Chapter of Legends of the Outdoors Hall of Fame. He is also the recipient of the LOWA's Arthur Van Pelt Lifetime Achievement Award in 2015 and the Sports Greats of North Louisiana Award in 2018.

Glynn is a member of the Southeastern Outdoor Press Association (SEOPA) and the Louisiana Outdoor Writers Association (LOWA) and served in leadership for both organizations. Since 1976, he has received more than 60 Excellence in Craft Awards for writing, broadcasting, and photography from SEOPA and LOWA. He also hosts four weekly radio programs including Glynn Harris Outdoors. He resides in the piney woods of Lincoln Parish with his wife, Kay, and their beloved dog, Coco.

Connect with Glynn on Facebook.

Made in the USA
Columbia, SC
26 December 2024